T0171485

NEPTUNE MOON

getting your energy in-tune

Trishe Jaimes

BALBOA.
PRESS

A DIVISION OF HAY HOUSE

Balboa Press books may be ordered through booksellers or by contacting:

Balboa Press
A Division of Hay House
1663 Liberty Drive
Bloomington, IN 47403
www.balboapress.com.au
1-(877) 407-4847

ISBN: 978-1-4525-0667-8 (sc)
ISBN: 978-1-4525-0668-5 (e)

Because of the dynamic nature of the Internet, any web addresses or links contained in this book may have changed since publication and may no longer be valid. The views expressed in this work are solely those of the author and do not necessarily reflect the views of the publisher, and the publisher hereby disclaims any responsibility for them.

The author of this book does not dispense medical advice or prescribe the use of any technique as a form of treatment for physical, emotional, or medical problems without the advice of a physician, either directly or indirectly. The intent of the author is only to offer information of a general nature to help you in your quest for emotional and spiritual well-being. In the event you use any of the information in this book for yourself, which is your constitutional right, the author and the publisher assume no responsibility for your actions.

Any people depicted in stock imagery provided by Thinkstock are models, and such images are being used for illustrative purposes only.
Certain stock imagery © Thinkstock.

Printed in the United States of America

Balboa Press rev. date: 09/13/12

Contents

This book is dedicated to my family and my good friends that I have meditated with over the years.

Introduction

The clock read three am and the room was filled with light. There was a strange yet calming silence as the glow within the normally dark room felt strangely comforting. The blissful calm was momentarily interrupted by an instant state of shock as I realized there was a being standing before me. The being glowed of pure light and seemed to touch the ceiling, the facial features were easily distinguishable, with an unusually rounded and ancient face. The presence felt male and his kind eyes gleamed with all the knowledge and wisdom of the ancients. The being raised his arms, outstretched above and across me, which brought my attention to his white glowing gown with long sleeves, and the light that radiated from the sleeves where hands would normally be. The light seemed to raise me from my state of shock in preparation of the urgent deliverance of his message. The calmness once again engulfed me as the being spoke in a reassuring, slow deep voice, which immediately put me into a state of calmness never before known. "The words will be spoken, so the words will be written, so the words will be heard once again".

It was a kind of angelic intervention or perhaps it was something other than angelic, a spirit being from a realm or time gone by that I was yet to understand. It was the first of many encounters that followed, all of which had a sense of urgency in their tone. Following this experience I had many strange occurrences happen and unfortunate events that would alter my current existence to allow me the time to write the words that were being delivered to me in dreams, meditations and clairaudient communication.

These words that were given, were complex and not understood at first, it took a couple of years for the pieces of the puzzle to fall into place, then the meanings became clear, things began to unfold just as the messenger said they would. These are the first words, the stepping stones to tap into the source of divine ancient wisdom.

In a time long ago and long forgotten, there existed a highly advanced race, a race of above human height, and beaming with the radiance of pure light. Eventually the civilization ceased to exist on this plane, they have now returned as a more highly evolved pure spirit, they are making themselves known that they are there to help us from behind the scenes, helping us to connect to our pure state, and return to a state of peace and connection, a feeling of oneness with all. They exist on the realm of spirit and can only intervene in our lives with our permission, they emanate a pure, calm serenity about them, they are wise as they hold the wisdom of the ancients, they are the wisdom and they wish to share that wisdom with us.

Foregone and long forgotten in a time long before your own, where an understanding was reached to deny the truth, in this denial of all people a false hope was created, it became a way of life. Before this, little was known how to reach communication on a personal level, however it was known by a select few that choose to deliver this guidance and all it revealed for those who heard the words that came from an inner source of wisdom that became known as the golden key, upon which all was revealed to those who possessed it, along with this was a time of surrender, surrendering the truth to all those who sought to keep this truth unknown and unloved, surely and steadily this evaporated to the cosmos from whence it came. Now and in times to come it is being released upon the world in small portions upon which are being spoon feed to the minds that hear this call. All else known becomes all that which indeed is to know and understand by the masses, as it is released sparingly to the hearts and minds of those in need. Be certain in your approach as you begin to take on this journey of discovering this purpose, should you encounter upon that which holds dear, begin to insist on the process of replacement, replacing old ideals with that which holds true within your heart.

These are very exciting times to be alive. The great white beings are presenting themselves, engulfing us in a state of pure peace and contentment, stirring within us the urge to stop procrastinating and do what we know we are destined to do. As they speak their words of truth, a truth that has been withheld for so long, there feels to be a great urgency that their message be delivered, as many people discover their true path and origin or feel the urge to seek out their true path. We are becoming restless, as we no longer want to be forced to do things because we have to, we are beginning to seek out truth, to seek out our hearts desires, we need to let go of the things in our life that cause us pain and no longer serve us, instead focus on the things that bring us the greatest joys. Do not be weighed down by the burdens of life, seek to find your true manifesting powers, the powers that are rightly yours, and create your destiny. These words of truth are being delivered to many. The words will be written so the words will be spoken, so the words will be heard once again. The words of the divine ancient wisdom come to us as messages in the form of oracles, a way of directly communicating with them.

We are being offered a glimpse into a world which we will soon be our own; it comes with a feeling of elation as we glide along in a blissful splendor. For now we can only hold this glimpse for a short time as we learn to release that which is no longer needed in our life, in order for us to move forward, to ascend beyond our burdens, to master techniques of will and create that which is necessary for us to vibrate in the new light of ascension, to reach happiness and elation.

Chapter 1

New Beginnings

U sing your intuition and allowing loving guidance to point you in the right direction can set you on a most joyous path, learning to live and love your life. Being grateful for your life will allow you happiness, the more you focus on the things that make you happy, the more you attract this happiness into your life.

Anything is possible so long as your intension serves a higher purpose for all involved. Once you start working with your intuition, it becomes very easy to accept and trust the guidance that is there to help you take the easier path in your life. As with anything new, there can be uncertainty about the unexpected and unknown, you need to trust that the new energy will become easier the more you work with it. Allow yourself the opportunity to open up to new awareness.

Living an abundant life is more than just manifesting what your heart desires, you want to live the best, happiest and most rewarding life that is possible for you. Using your intuition and allowing loving guidance to point you in the right direction can set you on your most joyous path, learning to live and love your life, being grateful for your life will allow you some happiness, the more you focus on the things that make you happy, the more you attract this happiness into your life. As you read these words and ponder upon the many gifts and opportunities available to you, please take some time to write down anything that happens around you, relating to your questions and your own development. Because with every amazing event that occurs, when you record it you are building your own evidence manual, this is the evidence you need to believe in yourself and your ability to receive the messages that come to you and to help you develop or understand your inner vision or voice. You may be feeling a blockage, fear or misunderstanding whether you are a beginner or have been trying for years. For you to have any chance of successfully connecting to your own gifts, you need to allow yourself to believe that you do have the ability to clearly hear, see, feel and know that you do have assistance in your life to help you improve your life and intuition. Everyone has these gifts or abilities, as well as their own unique gifts and talents, you just need to believe in yourself, trust yourself, even if it seems irrelevant, you need to understand the many possibilities. Once you start allowing yourself to open up to all that is happening around you and within you, you will begin to appreciate what is unique within you. It is easy to brush off another person's words or accounts but when you have experienced it for yourself, there will be no turning back. Experience and you will believe.

Some of the exercises in this book can be done in a group situation as sharing and building energy together can help everyone learn much quicker, all of the unique personalities and special gifts help to raise energy. It is important to be happy for any person in the group that experiences spiritual growth, as it will not happen for each person at the same time and your gifts will not be the same. It is like walking a stair case together, some in the group might seem to leap the steps, while others walk more slowly, and then the walkers will leap, whilst the leapers walk.

Call to those around you who you are comfortable sharing the growth experience with, as this will be the beginning of a period of growth and development.

"Humble beginnings are no barrier to achievement" I received these words many years ago through a daily inspiration card. It was at the time of a great transition in my life. It was just prior to my spiritual awakening and the realization that there was help available; I just had to know how to accept it. I had some very hard years in my life where I had very little, and very little to live on, I was just waiting for the world to hand me a break on a silver platter. I was never handed that silver platter, instead I came to realize that if I wanted a better life I would have to do something about it myself, so by putting effort into motion my life began to change. I started to meditate and began connecting with my guides and since that time they have helped me to make many choices in my life through messages and signs, so that my life could improve. So whilst I prayed for a break or an easier life, I was given the option and choices so I could make the improvements myself. You have free will so can choose to ignore this guidance, but if you knew that it would help you, why would you ignore it? Many people do receive help from their guiding spirits; however they do not acknowledge or recognize the help. Once you start asking for solutions, you need to be aware of the choices that are being given to you, as well as the coincidences and little signs that happen around you. The way I look at things is if an opportunity is presented to me, I take it because there is always something to be gained from it, whether it is a lesson or step in the right direction. I have always been truly amazed and forever grateful for the opportunities given to me. On the other hand if you feel like you keep banging your head into a closed door, than clearly you are on the harder path, taking the more difficult route.

I once had my deceased grandmother appear clearly in my mind and gave me a clear message about a job my husband was to take; giving me insight into something I could not have known. My husband was working as a contractor, which meant that his job could end at any time, his work colleagues around him had been receiving permanent positions with other companies, and while he was sending in applications and resumes he was receiving no feedback. He was becoming very downhearted because he is good at his job and felt as though he was being overlooked. I prayed endlessly for him and asked my guides for their help. Then I realized that our fax machine was not working properly, so all of the companies he was sending to did not receive his application. Obviously they were never meant to receive his application. So when we finally did get an application in, he received a job offer. This was a great boost to his confidence, as he was told that if they had received his application months ago he would have had the job back then. So while he was very happy, because many of his colleagues had already started with this company, it was very hard for me to tell him that he was to decline the offer. I received this guidance before he received any offers, "he is not to accept the first offer, no matter how tempted he is to take it, he should not. There will be a different offer within two weeks that will be better job security". At that time there were no offers, so when the first offer came my husband was extremely tempted to take it, in-case there was no other offer, I insisted that he didn't, I felt very strongly and had come to trust my guidance whole heartedly. Ten days later he received the second job offer, and he is still in that job now. The company is a larger company and many of his colleagues from the other company have since had to find work elsewhere.

There are many ways in which you can receive help; however it is important not to specify how or where the help comes from as this will limit the options. Instead trust and believe that if it is meant to be, it will happen. I do believe anything is possible so long as your intension serves a higher purpose for all involved. Once you start watching for the signs and noticing your own feelings it is very easy to accept the guidance that is there to help you take the easier path in your life.

The vision of my grandmother appeared in my mind as I was travelling in a car. The words flowed through my mind as if I was hearing them. Within two weeks the encounter was validated.

Chapter 2

ESTABLISHING A SENSE OF PROTECTION AND SECURITY

As you journey upon your path and make decisions and inner discoveries you may discover that your new hopes are different to the hopes of your present. It may appear that not all in your life would be as you planned and you may find it hard to disagree with the notion that you may want to change how you feel about your life and all that it involves. This will be a kind of awakening, as you feel your hearts true calling. There may be a period of feeling restless and unsettled in your current life role, in time you will become settled in your way of thinking and believing. It is very natural to feel as though you are not on the right path, or have some inner conflict or confusion as you know there is something you should be doing, but not quite sure what that is. Slowly as you begin to balance your life you will start to get a feel for what you want to do, what you should be doing or just have a feeling that you are on the right path. This will be the way in which all good things that are supposed to be in your grasp will soon begin to appear. There is no way in the short term that this can be resolved, you will need to approach each stage as it is presented to you, and this will only happen at a time when you are ready to appreciate what is being given to you.

Your guides bring forth messages of truth, joy and love, you are supposed to set forth on your journey without denial of the truth within, faith comes in many forms and without doubt, there is a spark of interest that blazes from within and sets you forth on boundless conquests and achievements, keep in mind that when you become like a child exploring, developing and accepting your abilities it will be the beginning of your true journey.

Everyone has their own belief system, and belief systems have changed over many of thousands of years. Externally we are evolving to understand what is internally felt. As you receive insight and develop your gifts it is very important to attribute your blessings to God, your higher self or your guides, always be thankful and grateful for what you receive. Do what feels comfortable to you, as long as it is for the good of all involved. Keep your ego in check, or you just might find that you do not receive anything else. Attribute your protection, and thanks to God the creator and protector, as you start to receive your own messages from your highest of guidance and loved ones. Although I am uncertain exactly what the divine protection is, I do feel that there is some greater cosmic power than what we see with our eyes and I feel safe with the feeling that I am always surrounded by divine energy. Once you feel that there is more out there you begin to feel safe knowing that you are protected. There are many things that you will encounter that you do not see with your physical eyes, just because you do not see something with your physical eyes it does not mean that is does not exist. Even though I have always believed in God I was given some clarity on the subject that put my mind at ease. I randomly posed a question to my guide "are you the one who protects me", meaning the one who has protected me from tragedy in the past, and the response was "no". I was a little shocked at the bluntness of the response, so next I asked "do I protect myself", meaning when I surround myself in white light, the answer was strong and powerful "no". Just then I had a light bulb moment, and I cannot explain where it came from, but the words I heard loud and clear were "God, God protects you", and from within I felt a true knowing, kind of like saying to yourself of course that is correct, it feels correct, it feels true and comforting to me. I feel very comforted by the fact that I am always protected by God, as is anyone who asks through prayer and appreciation, and it is this understanding that allows me to look deeper into the things I do not understand whilst feeling safe and protected.

The first thing you should understand when practicing meditation, guide connection, chakra balancing or any other form of spiritual learning you should always perform a white light blessing ritual that you feel comfortable with, I use a short prayer and visualization of myself and surroundings being saturated in white light. Visualize yourself shielded by this white light and ask God and your guardians to protect you from negativity, this not only serves as a form of protection but helps raise your energy. Some people like to circle themselves seven times, I feel comfortable and safe visualizing myself being completely surrounded and illuminated in white light, with it connected to a higher power or universe and surrounding and filling my environment. Visualizing the process is very important, and adds power to your intention. You may prefer to use a golden divine light or a pink light of unconditional love, which will shield you with love and keep out negativity. Or use the pure white light for protection then visualize a pink light for love. I use a simple prayer before beginning every meditation, chakra balance or connection process. You can easily change it to suit yourself. You must visualize this process as you recite it.

My personal white light blessing ritual goes like this:

I ask God to surround me in the pure divine white light of love and protection and ask that it surround my environment, home and car and everyone around me. Please allow this divine light to purify my aura and raise my vibration so I can receive clear messages from my highest of guidance, guardian angels and loved ones and ask my gate keeper to allow only messengers with the highest intent of love and truth to clearly communicate to me the knowledge I am ready to receive. Amen

I also give thanks to God on a daily basis for every opportunity that is presented to me, and I thank my guides for giving me the guidance that I need as I walk each step in my life. The more you are thankful for the more you will appreciate your life, and the more you will receive. When you are truly thankful you will receive blessings and miracles in your life and you will truly love and appreciate the life you have been given.

The saturation of white light will increase the energy flow emanating a higher vibration. To help you with your pursuits it needs to be reached in the conscious mind to allow for a transition into your relaxed state to be peaceful and clear. This should be started immediately and will allow for a higher flow and input of information. So before you begin anything else, learn how to feel safe, relaxed and raise your vibration using the pure divine light of love and protection.

An important thing to remember, especially if you are a beginner and do not yet have clear clairvoyant or clairaudient abilities, you are relying on your gut instincts so you must learn to trust it, as it is better to be wrong and not do something than to ignore your instincts and put yourself in harm's way. This applies to your everyday life as well as working with spirit guides. If something feels obsessive, makes you feel sick, confused or anxious, then you have the power to say no, I am surrounded by Gods love and only work with the purest of intensions. If you feel uncertain, do not have fear, ask your highest guidance or angels to stand close to you and protect you, then visualize your white light blessing ritual, stay focused on your ritual from start to finish then you should feel much better. This also applies to any situation in life, if it makes you feel sick, confused, anxious or uncertain, call your guides close to you and focus on your white light ritual, and ask what you best to do in this situation. The words or feelings will be loving and helpful. The work of a medium sometimes involves feeling the pain, ailments and sicknesses of those you are bringing through or those you are reading for, however this sickly feeling is very different to the feeling of negativity that is felt in the pit of your stomach when something is wrong. So if you find that by developing your gifts you develop an interest in helping others by working as a medium between our realm and the spirit realm, you will come to understand your own feelings as you will be working very closely with them, as you will with any spiritual gift you begin to develop.

Negative feelings such as fear, doubt, jealously and anger are also indications that things are not right or not as they are supposed to be. As you practice these exercises you will learn to let go of the ego based feelings so you can start to vibrate on a much higher level of love and inner peace. Your instincts and emotions will be your clues to your wellness and security. Fear, anger and negativity are things that we should try not to give thought to.

Always remember that you have free will and you are in control of how you feel. Always know that you are safe, you are protected and you are surrounded by guides that want to help you. You walk in divine light, you are protected and you are safe. As you become more in-tuned with your body and emotions you may find that others are drawn to you for your energy. This is why when a friend dumps their emotions on you, you can feel down or negative for no known reason, keeping this light around you will help. When you feel sick, angry, frustrated or any other negative feeling you need to sit with that feeling for a moment and acknowledge where the feeling is coming from. Has something happened that would make you respond in this way? Or is it out of the blue for no reason at all? If you cannot find a physical reason then there would be an energy based reason, perhaps some-one close to you is dumping their negative feelings on you or draining energy from you for their own needs, maybe someone you have spoken to or consoled lately. Once you have listened to your body and understand why you feel this way then you can do something about it. First acknowledge the feeling, try to understand where it is coming from, visualize white light surrounding yourself, then the person that is making you feel ill, this way they are connected to the divine light rather than connecting themselves to you, relying on you to fulfill their energy needs or make them feel better. Once you state your intention to connect to a divine energy and visualize this connection, then you should start to feel better. Ask your guides to help you clear away any leftover negativity and visualize white light being poured over you like a large jug of cleansing water. If you are not feeling well because of a physical situation, then you should take some time for yourself, surround yourself in the divine light, focus on your white light blessing and chakra scan and balance, finish off by visualizing your aura getting larger and brighter. If it is a medical problem, seek medical advice. All of these exercises are explained in more detail in later chapters. Once you have listened to your body trying to tell you that something is not right and acknowledged the feeling, it is unhealthy to hold on to the negativity any longer. Acknowledge it, and then let it go. Trust your guides and healing guardians to lift any heavy energy that is causing your uneasiness.

Prior to meditation you should be thinking about positive influences to help build your energy, you should not give thought to negative situations or people. Be very visual in your mind when putting the white light around yourself, others and the place you are in. State your intention of only working with those with messages of love and the highest intensions. If you happen to feel any doubt, concentrate on visualizing your white light ritual and trust that you are protected by your loving guides, continue this until the doubt is gone and the air feels light again. Spirit cannot come through, or help you in any way without your consent. Most importantly stay positive, working with purest intensions, and enjoy the connected feeling of working with your guides. If you are not feeling well, do not do anything too deep instead just focus on relaxing and breathing in the white light and healing any negativity that exist within you. Once you have finished, it is very important to share the energy that you have built up, with the universe, with those in need and with helping the environment. Your intensions are more powerful than you realize.

The first time I learned to notice the difference in energy was during a meditation where I was gaining knowledge from a very high realm, when I felt the presence of some-one else next to me, the presence was trying to get me to pass a message on to some-one else in the group. The high guide that I was receiving guidance from told me that this was a lower energy. I was shocked to hear it in such a way, as lower energy sounded so negative. I felt like I was in a state of tug of war between my guide giving me guidance and learning and some-one persistently wanting a message passed on. Eventually I thought it was important as a light worker to pass that message on to the person in need, as the scene of my high guide drifted away, I felt the energy change, I was back from my meditative state, but still relaxed enough to receive messages. The air was light, I felt as though I was floating and I was in a state of inner peace and contentment, it became a little heavier or denser. It did not feel negative and I did not have any feelings of fear, doubt or sickness. Lower energy just meant that I was communicating with a very high guide or some-one from an angelic realm to then communicate with some-one else's deceased relative. The deceased relative had a lower energy than that of the high guide but higher energy than my normal constant energy. Once you practice meditation techniques you will feel the energy around you rise or become denser, then when you have finished the meditation it will return to normal. The higher you can raise the energy, the higher the realm of communication. Practice feeling the energy when you are sitting with a group of friends prior to meditation and again after meditation. As you are sitting in a circle, hold your arms comfortably out to the side have your left palm facing up focusing on receiving energy and your right palm facing down focusing on sending energy. Each person in the group is to do the same, so the person next to you on your left hand side will have their right palm facing down sending energy and your left palm will be facing up, slightly under their palm receiving energy. Notice any feeling of heat or tingling and try to focus on building the energy so that you can still feel it as you slowly separate your hands. At the end of your group session hold your palms up and visualize the extra energy being sent to heal the universe, astral realm and any person that needs it. It is far better to send this energy to where it is needed than to have it stolen by any one on this realm or another. Energy can also be built by prayer, thinking of the loving situations in your life, the connections you have with your guides or people around you and your intension of helping others. Feel it build in your heart and surround yourself and others with this love, and as everyone else in the group does the same, you will feel the energy grow as the air around you thickens and warms. The energy comes from your heart and intensions. It starts in your heart centre through love, increases as you connect to the universe through the crown, and is given further power from the solar plexus power centre.

Whilst it is important to shield yourself it is equally important to look after yourself, start to take notice of the types of things you are putting into your body, try to avoid stimulants such as nicotine or caffeine prior to meditation and do not do any of these exercises if you are under the influence of drugs or alcohol. It is also important to drink lots of water, to prevent you from getting a headache.

Fear not that thou will seek in the presence of the lord".

Chapter 3

ACCEPTING GUIDANCE
TO IMPROVE YOUR LIFE

Y ou can receive guidance in many ways from your own body to help from other realms. Once you start working with guides and your own senses you become more comfortable with where the information is coming from. Below is how I have experienced contact and how it feels to me.

Spirit guides

Spirit guides are those beings that have lived on our earthly plain at some time. There are many and they are varied, they change throughout your life depending on what stage in life you are at and what lessons you are learning as well as what you are currently doing with your life. They are male or female, they are sometimes known to you, sometimes not, and they are sometimes a relative that has passed over that you may or may not have known in the past or past life. They all have different mannerisms, personalities and different ways of speaking. Your guides take you through meditations and help you with your stages of learning. There are guides for writing, guides for creative arts, guides for learning, guides for teaching and guides for problem solving, just to name a few, and you can have many guides at one time, helping you with different areas of your life. Some stay with you until the activity, project or stage of life is complete or changes. Guides can by deceased relatives and they can be those spirit who have undergone much training to become spirit guides, there are also those who have ascended to become masters with much knowledge to teach us. I feel the best way to describe their communication type is by telepathy; they portray their message with words that are understandable and that you can relate to. Sometimes the words are poetic, complex or have an ancient feel to them. They can also use music in your mind, thoughts, symbols and signs around you. You may even sense their anticipation and excitement of being able to have their message heard. They offer helpful insight, the messages are always offered in a loving manner and always for the greater good, or answers to questions. The answers can appear in unusual ways like words in a conversation on television or a brochure in your mail that is strangely very relevant to your current situation.

Communication can sound like what you would think is your conscience. One of my guides is from a very ancient past life that has chosen not in incarnate, instead he continually guides me through every incarnation. I have included more information on him at the end of this chapter. One of the most vivid encounters I remember having with my guide was when I was saved from a near tragic accident. I was walking across a road, there was no traffic, everything seemed to be in slow motion and I felt like I was in a bubble. I had the strangest feeling that I was about to be hit by a car, just then a car horn sounded and I froze on the spot thinking, this was it, I was about to be hit by a car. At that same moment a large car came speeding around a corner onto the road I was crossing and if I had not frozen on the side of the road I was on, I would have been right in the path of the oncoming car. The car horn that warned me was a car alarm coming from a car parked on the opposite side of the road, which had triggered for no apparent reason. I accept that this amazing experience was my guide, guarding me from an accident that was unnecessary for my life's purpose. Your main guide is with you throughout your entire life, and with you long before this life, this is why at first you feel like it is your own conscious because this sound is so familiar that it just feels like your own conscious.

I once had both my computer and backup drives fail on me within an hour of each other. I was devastated and in a complete state of panic, so I prayed for help and trusted that I would be looked after and everything would work out for the best. I then began to clean house because this is the time I receive the most vivid messages, when cleaning with water or doing something mundane. I was asking my guides, guardians and God for a solution to my very big problem. I was playing the radio as I tried to relax my mind. I began reminiscing because of the song that was playing on the radio. My guides were leading me (via reminiscing) to a town that I once lived, I was startled when I realized what was happening because one of the files that was lost belonged to a customer in this town, which made me think of this person. I said that I preferred to not give thought to this person at this time, so I was told that they would find another way to tell me. Sometime later I received a clairaudient message "a savior will come when the bell chimes one", I knew this meant 1pm, I did not know which day, or how I would be out somewhere near a clock tower at 1pm, then I was told "it will not be as you think", (clock tower), immediately the phone rang once and stopped, so I thought maybe a phone call at 1pm. Sometime later I received a call from a friend giving me an address of someone that could help and it just happened to be a street across from where the client lived that I was earlier reminiscing about, it turns out that by reminiscing with music my guides were visually leading me to this clients house because the place I was supposed to go was only one street past. It was now 12:40pm when I arrived at the address. At exactly 1pm I was told that the files were retrieved. When I returned home I thanked my guides, guardians and God and the reply was "How happy is thee that does believe". Also that morning I was feeling that maybe the two crashed drives was a sign that I was to change paths, and I was feeling the urge to write this book.

Guidance from your own body and emotions.

When you first begin, or even long before you have decided to turn your attention inwards, you have your gut instincts, such as when you have a strong feeling to take a series of turns in a place unknown to you and you end up in the place you were meant to be, or you walk into a shop for no other reason than you are just there at the time, and you feel like to must walk in, but there you find the item that you have been searching for, for weeks. Or when you find yourself staring at an item or have the urge to pick it up, only to find that during the coming week the item is something you need. From my experience this valuable little signal only needs to be regretfully ignored a couple of times before you learn to purchase the item because you are going to need it. So these resonate in the pit of your stomach as strong feelings, impulses or urges. You will find that as you begin to clear and balance your chakras, in particular the solar plexus chakra that your instincts become much stronger, and it only takes a few times of acknowledging their accuracy that you decide that your should trust them every time. Chakras are explained in the next chapter.

Your heart chakra, resonates or vibrates as your body is trying to communicate to you, just as your solar plexus or stomach area has a strong instinctual feeling, your heart chakra also has a similar feeling, however you feel it a little further up and it feels more like excitement, but not the kind of excitement that is felt in the sacral or sexual chakra it is more like a love, anticipation or excitement kind of feeling. So the chakra system is very powerful in alerting us to many exciting and also dangerous situations, this is why it is very important to listen to your body, which mostly vibrates in the major chakra centers, and each centre has a different feeling and a different meaning.

Loved ones on the other side

Loved ones on the other side often bring loving, supportive messages, their image appears in the mind as a thought or picture, or your will hear their voice in your mind, their voices sound the same as they did when they were here, even though the sound does not come from the physical ears. It is possible to see a loved one standing before you as if they were still here, but this will not happen if it is something you fear and just because it does not happen this way does not mean that the experience is any less real. Voice tone, personality, accents, and the difference between male and female is no different to speaking to a male or female living person. If they were bubbly and outgoing in life then that is how they appear or sound. If they were tricksters, then they still will be and you will feel like laughing. When you accept that it is possible, or that what you feel, see or hear is real than it will happen more readily for you.

Signs from spirit

These are happening around you everywhere and can occur in many ways from overhearing a conversation, or channel changing on a television, number plates on a car, flashing signs, dreams and any other numerous ways.

During my time writing a book, I posed a question if it is something that I should be doing. For two weeks whenever I turned on a television, at that moment there would be someone talking about writing a book, publishing a book, book editing or authors, this would be on movies, documentaries, talk shows and occurred every day for two weeks. I would see "book" written on car signs, such as book binding, or mobile libraries and even in the bushes on the side of the road was a hand written sign that said "book covers". After the book was written, I asked if I should do something with it and within two minutes there was a bright sign on a car beside me that read "be seen", the car radio played the words "I want you to know who I am", and a flashing sign said "talk of the town". It was obvious that others needed to see and hear the words.

When putting the details together for the second book, I put it out there to my guides what should be included. In front of me were two cars with number plates MU, which represents a Lemurian guide that I have. I always like to have three signs, within five minutes of asking for a third sign I walked past a car with cow seat covers that said moo. I asked what else should be included and a car went in the opposite direction that had the word Solar written on the side of it. One of the power energy raising techniques shown to me by a guide is called sol la. When I asked what else, a car pulled in front of me that had the word Buddha on the back. These signs were received almost instantly, from the moment of asking, sometimes it can be sometime during the day, for all the pieces to come together. I thanked my guides for the signs, at first I did not realize what Buddha meant, but a friend pointed out to me that it represented ascended masters, which I had been working with. These are just examples of how great and clear the signs can be when spirit wants to get an answer to you, Sometimes it is easier for them to communicate in this way.

One week before the appearance of my guide, I had a dream.

I traveled with a tall stranger (guide), he seemed to be leading me somewhere important. I looked around to read the signs, it said Indian Ocean. I trusted that we would get to where I was supposed to go.

There were small clues, dolphins, and a beautiful boat with a window below deck shaped as a dolphin that looked out to the ocean. I said "I can have this boat if I really want it" (manifesting). We came to the end of the road. We were surrounded by water with a footpath on each side, we went over a bridge. In the water stood what looked like large round buildings, but they were machines with cranes coming out, building things like bridges and roads. There were people inside of these crane buildings. The machine was laying new pieces of road before me as we travelled along. It was a new path that was being laid before me, I was very nervous as each piece was laid for my journey but I went along with it. As I travelled along the road with this guide I could see people on the footpath and swimming in the water. I was clutching three things being very careful not to drop them in the water. One was a phone account, that I did drop in the water but as it floated by I asked a young girl to pick it up for me. Another was an envelope and the last was a large thick document that was very important, it was like a typed plan or manuscript of some type. Once the road was complete my guide held my head under the water and said "you are first to see the ocean floor". I was nervous at first about having my head under water but trusted that it would be ok. The ocean floor had a thick uneven crust. The water was shallow, clean and clear. At the end of the journey I stood up in the water, I was not holding anything; I realized that what I had to give was very small in comparison to what I received. A chalkboard read I for the big white 1111 1111 1111 1111 for the great white. There was a song being sung, something to do with personality and being individual and true to self and some one that other would imitate.

Who is the great white?

Almost three years after having the dream of the great white, I decided to ask "who is the great white". I have had many recurring dreams were the tall white being leads me to a large room along a corridor for training. I remember when I am there that it is something that I was once good at and I am told that I am a star child. So I believed for some time that the tall white being is my high guide somehow connected to the training and perhaps a star being of sorts. My description of the white being matched the descriptions of others peoples angelic encounter. So maybe he is a star being or maybe he is an angelic being or maybe it is one in the same. It still feels unrealistic to use a title like this, even though angels are very accepted by many, whatever he is the event happened and he feels very realistic and has helped me in many ways.

So finally after many years I asked for signs to tell me who this special being is, and this I how I discovered the story of Lemuria.

Lemuria was a place, said to be somewhere in the Indian Ocean, now on the ocean floor, between Australia and Madagascar, incorporating the Easter Islands. It was said to be inhabited by an advanced race of tall white light beings, seeded by beings from the stars. Many old cultures believe that star beings came down.

Their race failed, apparently from abuse of power, or maybe it did ascend. Some say it was our 1st attempt at ascension that failed, Atlantis was the 2nd, and now we are the 3rd.

It was the first time I had heard the story of Lemuria, which I felt very connected to. The connections between the story and my dreams from the past few years amazed me. The Indian Ocean, below the ocean, first to see the ocean floor on my path, tall white light beings with advanced knowledge, and star beings. Also the dolphins are said to have a connection to Lemuria.

The story and the connections fascinate me to no end, but there is very little information about that lifetime, many lifetimes ago. So I am endeavoring to get it directly from my source.

Now for the validation, it is a very fanciful story, true or not I wanted to get further validations before taking it any further. That night I was awoken to a documentary on television about islands forming below oceans. For the next few days I saw MU number plates everywhere and my sons game avatar's name is MU and the final validation was when I had my aura photographed there was 2 long streaks of white light, a psychic told me that they were Lemurian beings that I had trained with in Lemuria, and they now follow me through every life. MU is a name that Lemuria is sometimes referred by, or MU MU land. Before this I had never heard of Lemuria.

Several weeks later I asked if I should write about Lemuria, once again I was bombarded by the word MU.

Onaahy, my dear Lemurian spirit guide.

"With you now and always"

Onaah is helping me move through doubt and be open to new opportunities. He says it is a whole new world that awaits my discovery. Secrets known but long forgotten will be remembered suddenly with great impact on my life. He cares much for all souls, but cares very deeply for my wellbeing and is proud and heartfelt to show me the way. He has been waiting eons for my awakening and feels much joy to my arrival and reuniting.

Onaah has a lovely sense of humor, he emphasizes the double a in his name and expresses that it does end in hy, but does not mind the shortened version of Onah. He jokes that I have always called him the tall white being, laughs and calls me the yellow girl.

I guess meaning that I am not really yellow and he is more than white light. He is a free spirit and seeks to enlighten me and thus free me. He reminds me of past conquests and endeavours that he has been through with me many times before but he is most delighted that I recognize him this time and acknowledge his presence. "Eons of time" he says, "It has taken you so long to wake up". I had done it hard by not realizing he was there to help me to remember him and allow him to help me as we had agreed many lifetimes ago in Lemuria. He says I did not have to go through them alone; he was always there, intervening countless times for my safety, without affecting my will or direction.

He shows me that we once both wore the uniform with pride. We adorned ourselves with much outer pride and self love, and much inner knowledge. He delights that I step into the light to once again adorn myself with truth. He speaks of honor, and much devotion that was taken to achieve the status we did.

"Please allow me to let you see the truth" that was manifest in our hearts, he raises his hand to show light radiating from his palm centre, reminding me that I too have this light but have forgotten how to see it. Within this light all directions of time can be known, all levels of creation are presented, it is all answers to all questions and can be read and understood, if I remember that I can see the light.

He puts a garland of crystal beads around my neck and reminds me that they resonate very deeply in my being at a soul level, they make me feel a little sick as the energy is stronger than I know. "Hold them in your palm then to your forehead, re-energise, re-open, re-member, who you are". I feel they may be connected to clear quartz, like an amplifier of energy or transmission. There is a Z shape on his uniform, representing the harnessing of lightning energy. He has healing abilities with radiant light, "as do you", he says, but it is not just limited to this. He speaks of motion, projection and alignment. The lightening represents the energy that passes from the sky to the earth and lights up the darkness. It is also passed from the higher to the lower parts of us and can be transferred from one to another. It is very energizing and puts light in any areas of doubt. I am an energy worker, just like he is, but still waking up to the capability. It is a very energizing feeling. He says that "this is sol la" means that this is the way. By harnessing light energy.

Chapter 4

BALANCING YOUR CHAKRAS TO BALANCE YOUR LIFE

What are chakras?

Chakras are your body's energy centers; they look like spinning discs that radiate colored light, they run down the centre of your body. Chakra is a Sanskrit word that means wheel. There are many chakras, however it is only the main seven that is discussed here, and a further two later in the book.

It is very beneficial to balance your chakras. There is a possibility that when you balance your chakras, the areas of your life that are out of balance will come to your attention. You may have disliking to the things that once took up much of your time and was out of balance with other areas in your life. You might find yourself starting to appreciate the value of self and how important it is to nurture yourself. Or certain problems in your life will arise forcing you to take action to balance your external existence, so that your chakras do not become out of balance again. I have also found that since clearing and balancing my chakras I can visualize and feel them easily and I can also feel when I am to receive a message. The most commonly known feel of a chakra is the gut instinct. This is your Solar Plexus chakra which is located above your navel. When you have a strong urge or feeling, or feel that something is not right you will feel it in this area. It can be a sickly feeling or a feeling like something big is about to happen.

The heart chakra is located above the Solar Plexus Chakra in the chest area; I often feel my heart chakra vibrate. One day as I was waiting to cross a road, my heart seemed to beat strangely, it was like a strong emotion, the best way I can describe it is like when you feel love or your heart strings are pulled when you watch a movie or read something in a book. This feeling seemed to happen for no reason known to me. Within minutes my husband was in a work car that I did not recognize, and was turning into the road I was about to cross, it seemed that my aura was able to pick up on his vibration close to me and make my heart chakra react. On another occasion, I was anxiously awaiting a parcel to arrive in the mail, I had no idea when this was to arrive as it was to be anywhere within one to four weeks. I was very excited about what I was expecting. On this day my heart chakra started vibrating wildly, it was for no reason at all, and at the time I stopped what I was doing and thought how strange that was. Within minutes the parcel arrived at my door.

It is not uncommon to feel a tingling between your brows when you start to work with your third eye chakra or a heating sensation at the top of your head from your crown chakra when you receive spiritual knowledge.

When learning your chakras, the names correspond to the area of the body where they are located, except the solar plexus, this is simple to remember by associating Stomach and Solar both starting with S, and the solar plexus color of yellow is the same as the sun (solar).

When I was first learning the colors of the chakras, I was uncertain of the colors so I thought I might go to the local paint shop to get color cards of all the chakra colors, so I would know the exact colors and where they were supposed to be. I did not make it to the paint shop because the day I was supposed to go the strangest thing happened. A circle of colors appeared on my wall starting from magenta up to violets, the violet was very hard to see almost invisible. The colors only lasted a few minutes and they came from the sunlight reflecting on a bike reflector outside of my window, I had not seen it before and have not seen it since, but it was all I needed to understand the colors of the chakras. It was amazing how the colors blended into each other. I have since learned that they are the same order that you would see on a color palette. Another interesting fact that I learned whilst studying photography is that when all of the colors of light are together they are pure white light. Black is absent of any color.

It is possible to view the light of the chakras, much like viewing the aura, refer to the chapter on viewing auras. It appears as pulsating light instead of being a constant stream of light, the easiest way to describe this, is like a funnel of colored light coming out from the area of the chakra, like that which comes out of a freezer when it is opened, but denser and a stream of light the size of the chakra.

I recently asked by my mother, if I ever feel so down that I could not even ask for help from guides, I could not answer yes as it had been a long time since I remember feeling very down. A couple of day later I had a number of things go wrong, leaving me with a very low feeling that I could not put my finger on the exact emotion or exactly why I felt that low, as I know that all of the things that happened were happening for a reason. I had this feeling for two days where I did not feel positive enough to clearly ask for help. On the third day I took twenty minutes out to do a full chakra scan and balance and discovered my base chakra was very blocked due to stress and worry. Immediately after the chakra balance I was back to normal. It is a good idea to do a chakra balance at least once a week, or whenever you do not feel quite right.

Start with the white light blessing ritual and ask to clearly visualize the chakras and have help from your highest guide to heal and balance them. It is important to be comfortable and undisturbed and breathe very slowly and deeply through the nose throughout the process. Visualize each chakra in your mind one at a time.

Try this exercise and give it as much of your attention and visualization as you can, stay with each chakra until you can see or feel that it is full and bright. This exercise is well worth your effort.

Start by visualizing white or golden light coming from God or the universe falling down upon you, completely surrounding you, and running down through your body, out of your base chakra and feet and into the earth, keeping you grounded. The light comes from within you, breath very slowly and very deeply as you scan and clear each centre, with every in breath visualize that you are absorbing the divine light around you and as you exhale visualize that you are releasing any negativity that you are holding onto. It can also help to use a clear quartz crystal near each chakra.

Taking very deep slow breaths through your nose, close your eyes and try to visualize your base chakra. Imagine a circle appearing in your mind and recognize this as your base chakra. Your base chakra is a deep red and may be blocked if you feel stressed, anxious, have fear based worries, money problems or problems sleeping. As with any of the chakras that you visualize, the circle may be very dark, and you may not even be able to distinguish it from the darkness of your mind. Stick with the visualization, focusing on visualizing a circle of red, holding the intention that it is getting clearer and brighter. You may start to see flecks of color, keep working with it until you can visualize a circle with magenta light streaming through, or your mind fills with the color.

Focus on this to make the blob, circle or flashes that appear in your mind, larger, clearer and brighter. The intention is to have all of your chakras equal in size and clear and bright.

Now focus on breathing in the white light around you as you move to your next chakra, the sacral chakra it is located below your navel and is a sunny orange color. Again visual it in your mind, it may be blocked if you are experiencing sexual tension, problems with addictions or creative blocks. Start with the darkness of your mind and focus on the intention of your sacral chakra appearing in your mind as an orange light, keep focusing on it until it is clear and bright and equal to the base chakra.

Again focus on deeply inhaling the white light and move up to your Solar plexus chakra, located in the stomach area; it is a bright sunshine yellow. This is important for instincts and will power. Visualize seeing it in your mind as a bright yellow and focus on the light coming from within you, pushing out any toxins until the color yellow pours out clear and bright.

Inhaling again see the white light moving up to the heart chakra, located in the chest area, as a beautiful emerald green. It is the place where you will feel love, empathy and a connection to your guides. You may need to release emotional blockages and will mentally need to surrender to the feeling of love and let go of any emotional turmoil in your life. Keep focused on the darkness of your mind, until this chakra appears as a very bright green light, green circle or blob in your mind, then inhale deeply and absorb the love that it has to offer.

Moving up to the throat chakra located in the throat area in a sky blue color. It is important for communication on all levels and clairaudience. Stay with the visualization until your mind is filled with bright sky blue.

Deeply inhale the white light around you as you move further up to your third eye chakra, located between your brows. It is a darker shade of blue, with a tinge of deep purple, indigo blue. It is important for clairvoyance and you may feel it tingle between your brows. You may also see a picture in your mind of an eye looking back at you, or blue clouds or moving blobs in your mind. Keep focusing on your mind until it is filled with an indigo blue or electric blue.

The last chakra is located on the crown of your head; it is the crown chakra and is violet/white in color. This is where you are connected to the universe and receive universal knowledge and guidance.

Once all of your chakras are balanced visualize a white or gold light coming from the universe running down through your chakras and into the earth. Now visualize all of the chakras radiating their colors and coming together around you, and forming the purist light color of white.

When you have finished you must remember to visualize them covered by the protective white or golden light, protecting you from picking up any negativity. Keep connected to mother earth and heavenly father. When you came to this earthly existence there was no point in your life that you had to open your chakras for the first time, just as your heart automatically knows how to beat, you did not have to turn it on. However over time, with all of the negativity around and life in general the chakras become blocked, just as your heart would become blocked if you kept polluting it with cholesterol. This is the reason they need regular clearing and balancing.

Chapter 5

AWARENESS OF YOUR OWN GIFTS

On your journey of self discovery you will find yourself questioning many things around you and the more you question, the more insight you will gain. You will no longer accept that life is what it is, nothing more and nothing less and the things that you have or do not have is the way it is going to be for you. Along this journey of self discovery you will focus on your senses as they are, and start to discover that they go much deeper. You will finally open yourself to you and all you are capable of. You may use these inner senses to further your current existence and material being, you may use the inner senses to help you with basic life decisions, however you may find yourself searching for balance and longing to understand your true purpose. All these discoveries should help you become a better person, assist your life in flowing better; most importantly you will discover your need to understand and trust yourself.

However you come here to this place where you now find yourself, feeling that you are meant to be here at this point in your life. You may be only at your paths edge or you may have already walked this path of spiritual awakening for some time. The words are to help you understand that you are not alone, and to help you find some meaning to why strange or coincidental things are happening around you. I share my experiences and experiences of others who have began their journey, in the hope that it may help someone else understand their own journey, and not to fear what they currently do not understand in the early development of your awareness of your inner senses. This should be viewed as a stepping stone to your true greatness and success in connecting back to you, allowing yourself to gain insight into your natural gifts and allowing yourself to find peace and contentment in your life. You will begin your quest for knowledge with much excitement and enthusiasm, as the more you practice and use your gifts the more happiness you will find in your life. You will soon discover the things in your life that are draining you of your life force energy and holding you down. The more you practice the balance techniques the more you will crave balance. The more you practice connecting with yourself, God and guidance, the more you will crave connection. As you have been drawn to the pages and the words that ring true to you, they will leave you with a feeling of contentment and curiosity as you seek your path to happiness and insight. As your awareness intensifies so will your lust for life and anticipation of miracles in your life. The meditation techniques are very basic and will allow you to delve deeper to find what works in your life, and how you can make improvements.

I found that as I started paying attention to my body's needs and listening to the insight that I was getting from my own senses, thoughts and feelings that many strange things began to happen. As I started to seek balance in my life, I soon started discovering the things in my life that were outweighing everything else. It was when the things that took most of my time went wrong for me, I realized how much time I devoted there, and I was able to see that other things were more important. You will be amazed at how many signs and coincidences there are happening around you every day.

The path is laid before you; this allows you to be guided on the path of self belief and understanding of the mysteries of existence. Keep an open mind to the signals and signs, as they are all around. The signs do point to the direction in which you are heading, so it is important to clearly read the signs, understand where they are leading, even if you cannot yet see the bigger picture or the destination, trust the inner guidance to know that you will achieve that which is intended. The crossroad does not end; the journey could be taken in any direction; however the duration and difficulty in experiencing that which needs to be lived and learned will vary depending on the path you choose, every decision you make influences your future. If something happens very easy for you than it is meant to be, if you seem to be continually trying to force something than maybe there is a better way for you.

A straight forward approach to believing is once you believe you see, you see. Or once you believe you know, you know. I don't want this to sound like "You will know it when you see it", as if it is going to be very obviously standing right before you within touching distance. This means that once you start believing in yourself and trusting yourself you will know that the tiny speckles you see in the corner of your eye, are actually you seeing spirit or that if you see something in your mind's eye, perhaps a vision of a deceased relative or a glimpse of a scene, then believe in yourself because it did happen, you did clairvoyantly have a vision, it was not just some silly thing that you can brush off as just your imagination. The more you believe in yourself, the more often it will happen and the clearer it will become. Is there any harm in believing in yourself if it makes you happy, after all isn't that what it is all about, your happiness?

Believe in yourself and all you are capable of. Believe in all the small things that happen around you, they are little signs from those who seek to guide you on your way. To fully understand that the potential of the mind goes far beyond anything we now understand, it is a depth that seems unattainable if you restrain your mind in its thinking, you have to work the areas of your brain that you do not normally work, you are opening up to your true potential, whilst we may never use our brain to its full potential, to just use it a little more than we currently do is to realize, how much more there is available. The most important lesson and exercise here is to believe that anything is possible and you do have the ability to achieve greatness and receive miracles, you do deserve the greatness, miracles and happiness. Be grateful.

Gifts and abilities are many and varied. You may desperately want to see an angel but it may not happen, instead you may hear the soothing voice of an angel or the insightful words of a guide, or deceased loved one. So while you may hear a lot clearer you may occasionally have visions or sightings. As you develop you will become aware of what you are better at, you can practice the other abilities which will be secondary to your main gift. Not everyone is a medium and neither does every one want to be, you may wish to develop your intuition solely for the purpose of making your life easier. Or you may find yourself wanting to become a teacher, healer, medium, revealer or councilor.

The following are some of the gifts that we each possess.

Clairvoyance—Meaning clear seeing. Clairvoyance is the most widely known that most seek to develop. When you hear someone say that they see a relative that has passed away standing next to a living person, they are using their clairvoyant gift. A clairvoyant vision is a picture or scenario that plays in your mind.

Clairaudience—Meaning clear hearing. This is where you hear a voice, or someone calls your name. It is clairaudient communication when a sentence of thought or names is heard in your mind even if you don't hear them from your physical ears.

Clairsentience—Meaning clear feeling. This is when you have a feeling in your stomach, or you feel an emotion or pain from another person. It is also when you have the ability to know things simply by touching or "feeling" an object.

Claircognizance—Meaning clear knowing. This is the gift of a psychic teacher or councilor that just knows what to say in all circumstances, they present an answer that they did not know they knew. It is a strong feeling of knowing someone is with you without seeing, hearing or feeling them.

These two gifts are slightly less common.

Clairalience—Clear smelling
Clairgustance—Clear tasting

The words were spoken: A fleeting glimpse, a warming of the skin, a feeling of knowing, a pushing urge to speak your mind, an acceptance and acknowledgement, the perception builds ever stronger as each instance is acknowledged, a belief in the unordinary and a knowing of an existence beyond our own. Take a look deep inside; understand the beliefs that ring true in your heart. You know that there is more to this life, this existence, have a self belief that we are all equipped with all senses that we need and that the senses delve deeper than the surface. Our hearing goes beyond the auditory, and vision beyond the here and now, it is a fine veil of light that opens to present a scene unlike the one it overlays. Believe that it is as it is presented to you, then that which is unclear will become clear.

Chapter 6

VISUALIZATION AND IMAGINATION

Imagination and Clairvoyance

It is a believing in your ability and trusting yourself, and an understanding that what you experience is truth and not a figment of the imagination. Is it possible that imagination is closely linked to how well you visualize and the clairvoyant visions you have? Imagination is something that as children we are told that we posses, and sometimes even frowned upon, such as over active imagination or imaginary friend, we are taught that in a practical world nothing is gained from imagination. Once it is relearned that imagination is magic inheritance, a gift that we all posses, than we can understand that all of our senses work together so we can hear, feel, see and know that there is much more to life than meets the eye. So this is why visualization and imagination are so very important to activate clairvoyance.

When I have a clairvoyant vision, it appears in my mind very similar to a daydream, except you are not really daydreaming, you could be reading something, walking, talking with some-one or doing something very mundane and your mind seems to play a movie, but you can also see whatever it is you are doing at the same time. It feels like there are two parts of the brain showing vision at the same time. The clairvoyant vision does not come through the physical eyes; it is in the mind like a daydream that runs on its own. Unlike a daydream where you can dictate what you want to happen or what it is you want to daydream about. A clairvoyant vision may only last a couple of seconds; this is also the way that some visions of guides can appear. So when trying to develop your psychic vision or clairvoyance, it is not all about what you can see physically like an apparition. The most important thing is that you trust that what you see in your mind's eye is correct, and not just your overactive imagination. I have had many validations to enable me to trust that my visions do mean something. Before a meditation I saw in my mind's eye, my guide walk over and stand beside me surrounded by a green aura. This was validated by another person that said they could see green mist beside me. In another meditation I could see my uncle in my mind's eye standing beside my mother and leaning in very close to her, he was trying to get a message through to her, he kept standing straight, then leaning down to her, and he was in deep concentration trying to get a message through. As he turned around and seen me it seemed to be a bit of a shock, as he was so enthralled in what he was doing, he did not notice me at first. So when he did notice me he said hello and told me he was trying to get a message through. Then he turned back around and leaned in very close to my mother. My mother new that he was trying to communicate with her, she could feel his presence, she felt as though he gave her a hug, and told her that it was because they never had a chance to hug before he passed. Also a third person viewed the aura of a person standing behind my mother from a distance. Prior to this happening, none of us spoke about my uncle being there, or requested a visit, there was no mention of him at all, he passed away only one week earlier, and he always said if there was way to make contact he would find it.

There are many ways that spirit can be felt, the energy around you feels denser and warmer, and when spirit stands beside you, you can feel warmth on your arms or face, my ears burn when they stand very close or sometimes I have muscle spasms or feel like I am being poked.

In my experience clairvoyance is like watching on an internal screen, viewing images awaiting your interpretation. To develop clairvoyance you must first release any negativity or fear of what you might see. You will not be presented with anything you cannot handle. I have had many apparitions and none of them appear as horrific as on the movies. In a meditation I was given the image of my soul star chakra being activated and connecting to the universe and also being connected to my third eye chakra. The soul star chakra is located above your physical body. I viewed the third eye as a physical eye looking inward viewing visions on an internal screen. The visions came from the energy that was being feed into my two connected chakras, the soul star and the third eye. The energy was like a whirlwind from the universe connecting to the light that streamed out of my chakras. This has greatly helped me understand and be able to view the internal glimpses easier.

The first glimpses of spiritual energy happened very early when learning to develop my ability. I remember catching a glimpse of little flashes of light, like glitter specs appearing on the wall. I remember asking my teacher what this meant, as I thought it may be headache related or that I needed glasses, my teacher had not experienced this to her knowledge, or maybe she had many years before and did not acknowledge it because it seemed irrelevant. So I just put up with it, wondering if I needed glasses. For the few years that I stopped meditating, the flashes disappeared and as soon as I began meditating again they came back. So I know for certain that it is related to spiritual development and sensing the presence of spirit. Now I see them whenever spirit, guides, angels and loved ones are present, I will usually see this prior to seeing auras or clairvoyant visions of spirit,

I experience it more frequently when my energy or vibration is very high. So if you are seeing specs you are on the way to clairvoyant activation. You may then begin to see larger orb like visions or faces. If you have fear of this then chances are it will not happen for you until you overcome your fear of spirit. Sometimes at first, when a vision appears before me, it can be a bit of a surprise and I do get a bit jumpy as it is normally unexpected, then I relax and try to communicate. There is no way that I know to force an apparition, their appearance has always been when I least expect it and usually during the middle of the night between 1am and 3am. Visions in the mind's eye can be on request, and appear simply by relaxing, stating that you want to see the answer to a problem, receive a message, have a visit from a spirit friend, or view your guide or the guide of another person. Look deep into the darkness of the mind, allow the bluish swirls to appear and disappear, moving in and out of your mind, this is very relaxing and soothing. This will either lead to a daydream type appearance in your mind or the swirls turn into a face or scene.

Exercise for the third eye.

Close your physical eyes start with your white light ritual and chakra balance to help you to relax, take in several long slow breaths. You may wish to listen to music and light candles and incense. In your mind's eye see the darkness of your mind without any images or thought. Begin to see swirls moving around in your mind moving in and out, expanding and contracting. Ask your guidance to present you with an image, focus on the swirls in your mind and know that once they swirl in and out an image will appear briefly in your mind, you may wish to repeat this many times, each time receiving a new image. You will find the more often you do this the easier and quicker it will become. Now after viewing this a few times, ask to view your internal eye. As the swirls come in then disappear, an eye should appear in your mind. If it is a closed eye, see it opening. If the eye appears blocked or blind you may not see it in full clearness, ask for help from your guides to clear this. You can visualize light from above pouring in through the third eye centre between your brows, see it washing around your internal eye and hold the intention of clearing your blockage or blindness. Keep working on seeing the eye in your mind. Once the eye has appeared in your mind, ask your guide to help you connect it to the universe to give you images to view in your mind. See a light above you, the bright light of your soul star chakra. Visualize a white light coming from the universe and passing through this soul star chakra and also coming down to your third eye chakra, visualize them connected, and feel yourself grateful that the universe will send images through this tunnel of light and into your third eye to be watched in your mind by the internal eye you have visualized. Give thanks for this wonderful gift whether it has been received yet or not. Be thankful that you were able to visualize the light coming from the universe connecting your soul star and third eye chakras.

AURAS

Auras appear around all living things. They are quite simple to see once you know how. The easiest way to start is to wait for an overcast day, sit in a comfortable relaxed state with a view of the horizon, or distant trees or mountains. Visualize your third eye opening and being very clear and bright. Now soften your gaze looking just above trees or horizon, in your sight you should see a white or light blue light around the tree or mountain, try not to move your eyes to look at it directly. It is easier to see by looking just above it.

To practice viewing other people's auras, ask a friend to stand in front of a clear or light colored wall and think positive uplifting thoughts. They can also speak about a spiritual experience or dream out loud. Now stand front on to your friend to look either into their third eye or just above them, try not to move your eyes too much. Again as above soften your gaze and try to see the thin white light around them, you might find that it pulsates and becomes larger in some areas. The more you practice the easier it will become and you will start to see colors or blobs of color in areas. Auras will change depending on how the person is feeling at the time.

You can practice with a photograph if you feel uncomfortable staring at people for a long time.

Visualization through meditation

In order to be able to successfully meditate you need to feel relaxed enough to let go, if you find you are seeing too much at once, or cannot seem to relax, you will find it easier to have a safe place that you can go and relax both physically and internally, make sure that where you are meditating is a place that you feel secure and are free of distractions. Where you go internally is to visualize a beach, a cloud, a garden or a place of worship and from here you can deeply inhale and exhale, putting yourself into a deeply relaxed state, to receive the information and guidance you need.

As you begin to meditate, clear your chakras or tune into your intuition, you will notice changes around you, so it is comforting to know that these things are normal and nothing to fear, you must understand that you are always in control of your own mind, body and senses. Let go of all fear, breathe deeply, relax and enjoy the time you have for yourself. Do not fear meeting your guides through meditation, just because they are trying to get a message through to you, it does not mean that something bad is going to happen, it is only that they are happy to communicate with you, and that you are finally acknowledging their communication and trusting yourself that it is very possible. Sometimes the heightened emotionally charged encounters can leave you with tears of joy, the strength and clarity of the message can be overwhelming. The overwhelming feeling also can also be from an emotional loving reunion with excitement on both sides. Once you start working with your chakras things should happen very quickly especially in a group situation where the energy build up is very strong. Sometimes when a message comes through it can be constant and persistent, until I acknowledge it. I find that when I am hearing something, the message can be persistent and repeated over and over until you acknowledge and say it, then you can move on to receiving more information. Another friend received a constant sh, sh, sh, being viewed in her mind after her first meditation. It would not go away until she acknowledged that it was a message for her. The strain of it all caused her to have a headache. This is why it is important to drink water and release extra energy to those in need.

You may be wondering why you cannot just jump into receiving messages, healing or working with guides or developing intuition, without meditating. Well you probably could, but I have found that meditating allows you to do it clearer as meditation allows you to clear your own energy centers, cleanse your aura, uplift your own spirit and raise your vibrations for easier communication. Apart from that, it leaves you feeling relaxed and uplifted; this should be enough to make you want to mediate. So even if you are having trouble meditating or visualizing, stick with it, your abilities in others areas will still develop, as you are relaxing your mind and devoting your time to learning from your guides in the spirit realm.

For some people it can take time to learn, so in the mean time relax and absorb the relaxing healing properties of meditation. There are many kinds of meditation, some people meditate upon and idea until a thought appears in their mind as an answer to a question, or to help make a decision. There is mediation for relaxing and there is meditation for spiritual growth. Whilst you are learning it is best to go with meditations that are very visual and descriptive and allow you to open up to the visualization process because these will stimulate this area of your mind. Allow your mind to wonder, you will often hear that you should not allow your mind to wonder, but by restricting yourself you are preventing your mind from growing and learning to let go. Do not struggle to close your mind off instead let thoughts come and go. Let go of any problems, this is your time to fly and your time to be free, the possibilities are limitless and you will have the opportunity to meet many guides and loved ones on your journey. So it is worth sticking with it, but do not be hard on yourself if you are unable to meditate straight away, you are being prepared and just by allowing yourself to enter a relaxed state and feel your vibration rise to another level you are well on your way to the beautiful journey and lesson for spiritual growth available to you. A blindfold can be helpful if you are distracted by flickering in your mind. A blindfold may only be necessary a couple of times. I also feel that by returning to your sanctuary any time you are struggling, automatically sends your mind into relaxation, and from here you may experience symbols or guides coming into your sanctuary, as this is where you are most comfortable. Another very important step is deep breathing through your nose, to switch your brain into relaxation mode. I also find that soft relaxation music allows you to go deeper with every beat and to limit any distraction, as silence tends to heighten every little noise.

The astral realm where you go when you meditate appears in your mind like a vision, you are not merely meditating and closing your eyes and looking into your mind. You are relaxing into a deep state of being where you are using your mind as an instrument to navigate and see what is there. It is not uncommon to see bluish specs or visions that appear as sparkly blue images, this is the energy of this realm. You may see clouds or shapes moving in and out of your mind, which is then followed by a clear vision of a scene of face, this is all very natural. It is also very normal for the scene or symbols or visions to change quite often. You might catch a glimpse of something very quickly or you may be able to hold the vision a little longer to delve deeper into the lesson you are being shown. It all depends on what is right for you at the time and only your guides can be a judge of this. However everything you see, no matter how small or quick holds significance and should be treated as a special gift of insight that you are very grateful to receive.

You may first just see a symbol, moving blobs or sparkling specs of blue, they may change into images and can appear quickly and disappear just as quick, however the image leaves a lasting impression in your mind which later you understand the full picture from a glimpse of an image. You may receive a very clear answer to a question from a kind voice of your guide that is there to help you on your life path, meditating will help you to hear your guides and allow you to exercise your third eye, which is responsible for your clairvoyant sense. Your meditation will become almost like a dream state, where you are shown and told many things the difference between your dreams and meditation is that you have little control over your dreams, with your mediation you are able to ask questions and ask to see or hear things clearer, you are free to look at any area of your visual journey. Like a dream, your vision will present itself without you having to think about what you want to see or do, but you have the free will and ability to make sure you have a clear understanding of what is being presented to you. You must always do this in appreciation of everything that is presented to you, and appreciation of God and your guides for allowing you the opportunity to learn. My very first meditation was at the home of some-one that I did not know there was a group of people attending and we each lay on the thin mattresses that were provided. The lady of the home guided us through, all I remember was my angel appearing to me very clearly in my meditation in the form of a childhood painting of Hansel and Gretel being guided through the woods by an Angel. My angel very clearly said to me "This is not right for you at this time, go away and try again at a later time". After coming out of the meditation I told the instructor of what I had seen and heard, and I was so lucky to have received this message because this woman turned out to be a little crazy, she would not let us out of her house until we sent the spirits to the light, they had some-one outside flickering the lights and she was yelling "tell them to go to the light". Well this was a very frightening experience for a beginner. So when I was able to finally get out of the house I ran to my car surrounding myself in so much white light so I did not take any of her negativity with me, even if it was all in her own mind. I did just what my angel told me to do, I never went back there again, a few weeks later I was introduced to a lovely teacher, and have enjoyed every experience since.

Meditation allows you to relax and focus your mind, it raises the energy level so your communication will be clearer, and it is also very good for eliminating stress and keeping a clear mind, so you can better deal with anything in your life.

It is very important that before a meditation you must think only positive thoughts, clear yourself of any fear, doubt and any other negative emotion. Do not speak of negative people or events and do not speak negatively about anyone. You want a wonderful, enlightening experience so you need to think enlightened thoughts. Focus on the closeness that you do feel or will feel with your guides and angels that are always with you and love you unconditionally. You must not be under the influence of any drugs or alcohol and try to have the least amount of toxins and additives in your body as possible.

Chapter 7

ACTIVATING YOUR CLAIRAUDIENT GIFT

Free writing

This is a subject of great interest to me and the main reason I feel so connected to my own guides and universal knowledge and able to receive clear communication. I have intentionally put it after the other chapters because it is necessary to first learn how to protect yourself, open and balance your chakras and find relaxation and focus through meditation.

There are many ways to receive this form of communication and there are also many names by which it is known, such as automatic writing and sealed writing to name two. I call it free writing because it is free of my conscious input.

The name automatic writing seems to imply that the pen picks up and goes on its own, it does happen this way for some, however for me personally; free writing comes from a source of knowledge and is relayed through me with words via my thoughts in a relaxed state, as if it is being dictated to me. It takes the entirety of my thought process and I am unable to perform any other task, think any other thought or be distracted by other noises whilst this process is happening. Normally I am a very good multi-tasker, but during free writing I am fully devoted to receiving the words one by one and immediately having pen to paper, as they come so fast that if you do not write them down straight away the message is completely lost, as it is not stored in the memory. It never ceases to amaze me how the words come out one by one and they all blend and go together when you read the information back, even though at the time of writing I have no knowledge what is being written. I feel strongly that this information comes from a guide and is useful information to be prepared for things that are coming up in life. I have clairvoyantly seen my guide, Guardian of Truth and Wisdom, pacing back and forth as he gave thought to the message he was about to deliver to me. My guardian always signs his name this way, and I never know the exact words or order of his title, even to write it now I had to look it up. But every time he signs off, it is exactly the same way.

When I first started free writing I would only receive three words at any one session and it seemed a strain on me to receive this, but slowly as I practiced receiving and built myself up for longer sessions. I now receive pages of information at one session. Over the years one of my guides would write in rhyming quatrains and I was amazed at how easy the words would come and rhyme with the words previously received. I have met others that also receive their messages in this way. Your messages can also come from loved ones on the other side; however their wisdom is specific to what they know, and the bigger picture of the situation you are in.

It is a very easy activity to do, you just need a book especially devoted to receiving messages, time alone when you will have no distractions at all and it does not hurt to have a ritual process such as lighting a candle or incense, this will indicate that you are ready to give your full attention to their message.

When you first begin you may only receive a couple of words, so be thankful to your guides for those words and understand that it takes time to become relaxed for long enough to receive messages, but always be grateful for what you receive. Don't forget to date the top of the page, you will find this very helpful and leave a blank page so you can fill in how these words influenced or helped you over the next couple of days. Eventually you can build yourself up to receive messages for likeminded friends and family.

Start by lighting your favorite incense, I like frankincense or lavender as I find these very relaxing. Next go through your white light blessing ritual, and ask that your session is blessed with only loving and helpful messages received very clearly. Ask to speak with your highest of guidance. Open and unblock your chakras so you can receive a clear transmission. If you cannot hear, ask your guide to speak clearer and louder. I also find a clear quartz crystal helpful in amplifying the signals, your crystal should only be used for this purpose, make sure it is cleansed in sea salts, charged in the light of a full moon, then you will need to program your crystal giving it the duty of amplifying your messages. You will not always need the crystal as you will soon attune yourself to receiving the messages clearly, but when you are starting it is great to have any help that is available.

If possible turn off any phone or distractions; sit in silence or with soft relaxation music. Now write down any word that comes to your mind, even if it seems unusual, I still sometimes receive unusual words, kind of like a sound check, "testing one, two", maybe they are checking that the words are being heard before the important message comes through, but they may be important so write them down. If I do not write them down I do not receive anything else until I do. You will need to completely focus your attention to this task and do not think about anything else just sit with your pen to paper ready to receive the words. When you think you have done enough, give thanks to you guide and to God, shield your chakras and close off. Try to start with a short amount of time and gradually build it up, if you sit too long in concentration before you are ready you risk getting a headache. You can specify how long you would like to receive messages. I always find that the transmission stops on the exact minute that I have stated. I sometimes write until the full message is delivered and my guide signs off, your guide will know when you have had enough. It is important to feel safe in the knowledge that you are connecting to a loved one or a close guide. They will normally express in words like you and your as opposed to I or me.

So you are familiar with the kinds of messages that can be received the following are examples and validations.

This next message was given to me the day before a meditation, at the time of receiving I could not understand it, but after the meditation when broken down it made perfect sense, the message is in italic. There would be two new people to sit in the group, this was unknown to me at the time of receiving the message. When I turned up to do the meditation I was a little shocked at the new people and I felt a little nervous as I knew nothing about these people. I did not know until the end of the meditation that one of the new people brought uncertainty and doubt from a past experience, but she left the experience feeling very relaxed with a renewed faith in how wonderful the experience can be. As I was requested to do in my message I visualized white light in the form of water pouring over the person to my right, and this person was able to have their first in-depth meditation. We had been experiencing an ever changing group with not every person attending every time.

A new world experience will begin a new challenge it is not out of grasp but you should try to overcome the feeling of pressure relating to new energy. (my own nervousness about new people sitting that I did not know, as well as being new to teaching) *Open the flow of energy as it may become blocked on the right side this should be remedied by picturing a white water streaming down over the area to cleanse any uncertainty creating negativity, this saturation of white light will increase the energy flow emanating a higher vibration.*(the person to my right was struggling, then had the best mediation she had ever had) *It is certain that I will be assisting the flow and watching over for over flow of energy it needs to be circulated from within.*(my guide was helping with the flow of energy around the circle to be equal and smooth and raising the vibration) *It should be known that there will be an uncertainty which will give a false sense of hope. I will give clear and precise information when this arises to relay to the person in need of assistance.*(one of the new sitters had a past bad experience in a meditation, so was harboring fear and doubt, and was pretending that this was the first experience of meditation) *Keep the answer clear but brief and do not be startled by the presence of another.*(the new people had questions about their past experience) because I had been pre-warned I was careful not to look startled when they explained their previous experience to me. *Call to those around you that are comfortable sharing the growth experience, as this will be the beginning of a period of growth unsustainable with a constant change of energy.* (This was a growth period for me, learning to put people into a meditation, and necessary to keep the same group each week) *We could allow for more information if we felt it was necessary to assist in the growth. The fear and uncertainty will need to be purified to allow for purer energy and this should be done by the healer.* (The healer of the group had done some healing in the room but had not properly cleansed the room)

Fear not that thou will seek in the presence of the lord. (Do not have fear or doubt)

This next message came to me when I was questioning whether I should write a book or not.

Only in the shadow of a doubt will you find your real challenge of staying focused. A journal writing of understanding your inner abilities, the possible cause of your happenings and insight, and a realization that you are more then you currently understand yourselves to be, in all that you are capable of. It is a combination of answers to questions and guides answers to your own questions, and includes all you have come to understand along your own journey and all that is possible that you are yet to understand. The journey unfolds as an enlightened path taken by those in search of truth and whilst the truth that is sought is different for all, it is about understanding your own truth and how to believe in yourself. At times you can all feel drained and exhausted and wonder why you put yourselves through the pain and heartache that you do, but it is about coming to an understanding of how you can learn from the things that happen around you, how to prevent things from happening simply by learning to trust that inner voice. This is a guide to your own soul, a realization that it is possible by trusting your own instincts, so simply by sharing your own insights of how you came to trust yourself will help others on their own search for inner truth and wisdom. In addition to the inner wisdom there is a universal wisdom that is available to all, in part and portion, as you accept yourself to receive it. But most importantly the first lesson is the understanding within, which can be used to heal a wounded soul, a broken heart, or set you straight so you do not need to experience the pain. For there is truth in the pain being unnecessary and once you understand that your inner voice can prevent your mistakes, and help you on to an easier path, then of course you would choose the easier path, if you knew it existed. So by understanding what is available to you on your journey, both in the material world and the things you need in life to make your life simpler as well as the inner tools that you possess to help you along the way. Believing in your own abilities is your first step in the enlightenment or wholeness process the primary reason for it is to find the hearts inner calm, and hearts true calling, so in seeking to find the inner peace your outer existence will vibrate on a higher level allowing you to feel true happiness which is in deep where the heart sense arises from, it is the higher vibration of inner contentment. The contact that you seek and curiosity of the unknown is a heart-filled connection that will allow your connection to yourself in the certainty of achieving learning and loving your true potential. The awareness that is found along the way is part of the gifts given to you in exchange for appreciation. Allowing the fulfillment of the heart will be established when you realize your gifts have been there all along, as you open your heart and mind to receiving.

A mindful knowledge and inner wisdom, allows a peaceful heart and a fulfilling experience. Amelio, Guardian of Truth and Wisdom

Clairaudient sound

As with clairvoyance where it can be an image that you see physically or it can be the images you see in your mind's eye. Clairaudience also occurs in different ways, senses are different for everyone, this is why it is so important to keep notes on everything you do, hear, say, think or feel, so you gain an understanding of how it works for you.

I have known people who have heard their name called, or a whisper in their ear. Your ears may become warm or go red. For me personally it feels like hearing it from a place in my mind that I visualize as being behind my ears. It feels like the same way the brain would process an actual sound, however the sound does not pass through my physical ears.

When I first began hearing it sounded like either telepathic communication or my own higher self, over time I have learned that the sound can sometimes be male or female, the words are sometimes slow, peaceful and soothing and other times it sounds like a very excited fast paced person. Tone of voice and accents are also comprehendible.

There are several exercises to perform to strengthen you clairaudient ability. Practice the free writing exercise regularly as this will help you be able to recognize when a message is coming through. Physically practice sitting quietly and listening to noises or conversations around you, focus on concentrating on a noise or conversation as far away from you as you can. This will help your focus and listening abilities.

Clear and activate ear chakras by visualizing three white pyramids, the two outer smaller than the one in the middle one, each of the pyramids is glowing white and has a beam coming from the point of the pyramids and connecting to the universe. The two outer pyramids represent your ear chakras and the middle pyramid represents the crown chakra, this visualization will connect your ear chakras to your crown chakra for clear communication from the universal realm of knowledge. The ear pyramids are connected to the crown pyramid at the base and they are all connected to the universal knowledge through the beams of white light. This is a useful visualization prior to the free writing exercise as it helps you become focused and relaxed and states your intention to connect to the realms of knowledge and wisdom. The visualization process is more potent and powerful then we can understand.

Chapter 8

ACCEPTING ABUNDANCE IN YOUR LIFE

Having abundance in your life leads you to have a happier more fulfilled life. There can be abundance of many things, happiness, guidance, love, security, prosperity or friends. There is a universal abundance available to us all, which is easily at our reach when we know how to ask for it and align our creation of abundance to serve a higher purpose. You do not need to be stuck in your rut if you understand that you do have guidance to help you with the things you need.

Being able to have material possessions and money to make life easier is not bad, life should be better spent than worrying about money. Money is necessary for most things in this day and age, and it can also be used to help others, so why struggle when there is enough universal abundance to go around, after all it is necessary for your everyday existence. I have learned to view money as a means of living, because when you do not have to worry about money you are able to get on with living. I trust that the universe will provide for me. I know this sounds easier said than done, but with persistence and belief things should get easier. I believe money will always be there when I need it, as I know that if I look after my life and my interests, the universe will find a way of making things happen as they are meant to be, so if it is to cost money then the money will find a way of presenting itself. I understand that money just does not fall from the sky when you need it. So you have to be aware of other ways it can present itself. It could be that you have the opportunity for extra shifts at work or that you take on a boarder, or you receive a promotion or pay-rise, all these things do convert to extra money eventually. It could also be that when it is really needed, you receive an unexpected refund, or money that is owed to you, you could sell something suddenly that previously you were unable to sell. You may find relief from your financial burdens by losing the desire for unnecessary spending, or things costing less than you anticipated. There are many ways in which you can receive help; however it is important not to specify how or where the help comes from as this will limit the options. Instead trust and believe that if it is meant to be, it will happen. I do believe anything is possible so long as you are not greedy and not only receiving guidance for material possessions. My guidance often helps me financially when I ask for their help. However I do not connect with them solely for the purpose of financial assistance. On one instance my bill account was short of paying all of my bills by quite a bit of money. I asked my highest guidance for assistance with this problem. Fifteen minutes later I received a phone call from a person that had owed me the exact amount of money that I needed. I had not seen or heard from this person in quite some time, and the money was owed to me for over a year. I received the money that day. Needless to say I was very thankful that my guides had pulled through for me once again, and it never ceases to amaze me and all of the people around me when this happens. Quite often I write a list of current expenses, only to find that cheques from various sources appear in my bank to the exact amount. On several occasions I have asked for certain material possessions, shopped for them, noted the exact amount of money needed, and received the amount from a job, or insurance refund or some other form to the exact dollar value of the item I was shopping for. There is power to writing it down, you give your desires a more concrete state when they are written in ink, it expresses your seriousness about the issue and not that it is just a passing fancy. Similarly a goal book or book that you stick pictures of your desires in works equally as well. The following exercise works very well for manifesting necessities in your life.

Believe—desire—express—accept—gratitude

First **believe** that you are worthy, that it is possible and there is enough to go around, and that if it is best for your highest good than it will be provided. Then have a clear picture of your **desire** and state that desire to your guides and angels, **express** its permanents by writing it down or have a picture of it. When you receive unexpected money or help in any form, **accept** that it is the answer to your prayers and most importantly, be very **grateful** for any and all help that you receive. Imagine a spoilt child, if you kept giving and giving to a child that never shown appreciation only a greedy want of more, then you would soon realize that this kind of giving is not beneficial to this child. However if the child was always grateful and thankful, then you would continue to give to this child as they are learning to receive graciously and to give gratitude in return.

Chapter 9

THE MOST IMPORTANT MAP DIVINE

As the planet Neptune follows it's map through the heavens and settles into the constellation of Pisces in 2012, where it will stay for 14 years, we will start to feel the changes in our energy and feel a desire to tune into these Neptunian energies, which are intuitive, and compassionate. This energy is responsible for our desire to seek the truth and our understanding that things are not as they seem or we have been lead to believe. Combined with the moon symbolism, we all have the opportunity to come out of the darkness with clarity to see the truth behind the illusion.

So finally after five years of following divine guidance, I begin to understand. Beginning with dreams of important paths and dreams of being shown tunnels of light leading to a large room where some type of education is occurring, along with urgent persuasions to do what needs to be done. The journey has taken five years, and when considering the star child dreams, it has taken much longer. I have held back for a very long time, but now the urgency has become too much, we are at a crossroads. But it is not the crossroads that we think. We have been lead to believe that we are at a cross road with how we treat the planet and to some extent this is right, however the most important thing that has been hidden from us, by the use of "slight of hand", is how we treat ourselves. All of the steps in this book have been directions toward the light, documented in the way they were instructed to me, but I could not see the light, I was blinded, but now I see. I thought it was about positive thinking and being positive but this is only a part of it and a very small part. Positive thinking is important, but divine thinking is more important. We have all been kept in the dark, and many of us on our journey toward truth and ancient knowledge have gone within to seek the answers, the key is within, however we have forgotten to look on the outside to see what is going on around us. The keys are within reach, to seek this truth yourself, but it is better understood if you seek the knowledge for yourself.

The directions that have been given are useful stepping stones but they mean nothing if you continue to live impure and disconnected from nature. You can balance your chakras as much as you like, sure it will make you feel better but what is the point of putting a band aid on your head for a headache, the cause of the problem needs to be healed. You are a healer, we are all healers. Start by understanding what you are putting in your body, do you really know what all of those big words are. If not, research them understand how they affect your body and your divine connection. Our divine connections are being severed and this is where the crossroads lie, we are existing within a heavy fog, a fog that has been building over time, as technology grows and all of these extra waves are floating around, they are damaging our own natural frequency. The frequency that we use to tune into nature and to connect with our divine helpers. Please do not take my word for it, and do not take anyone else' word for it. It is most important that you trust your own instincts for yourself. How does the idea make you feel? At first your instincts may not be so strong; after all you are clouded within the fog just like everyone else. But as you make the changes your connection will become stronger, and just like I was instructed five years ago. To begin replacing old ideals with that which holds true in your heart.

Ever since I was a child I did not like to drink water, I had an aversion to it and not just water, any fluid; I drank very little, did not thirst and would often dehydrate myself, which is very dangerous. I have since encountered a way to drink pure H2o, using reverse osmoses filters which remove all heavy metals from the water, it also removes chlorine and fluoride. The funny thing is suddenly I love to drink water, it was like my intuition guiding me not to drink the water. But once again, I strongly believe in what I have been guided to, but you must learn to trust your own guidance and not just follow what others tell you. The other thing that I have an aversion to is mobile phones, I despise using them, forget to carry it, and it is always flat. I know this annoys everyone around me, because I am so hard to get hold of, but I know that it is my intuition guiding me to avoid them. As you look around you, start to questions things, it just may open your eyes. There are many unanswered questions to consider; why is there so much cancer and depression.

Exactly twelve months ago to this day, that these words are written, I was given the 11:11 wakeup call, that many others have been given, I would hear it over and over again in my head "open your eyes", and the 11:11 would appear everywhere, I was astounded when I done a web search and discovered that I was not alone, many have received the call. However, just because you receive the call, the 11:11 that has been programmed within us to wake us up, does not instantly wake us from our slumber. It has also just occurred to me that there may be a connection to the dream that I had five years ago "1111 1111 1111 for the great white" and the 11:11 wakeup call that I started receiving twelve months ago. Another strange coincidence, I have used the number 323 as a sign to mean publish books for about two years, it was shown to me by my guide that this number would indicate publishing, the strange coincidence is that I have submitted the manuscript to the publisher on the 3rd month, 23rd day. I did not plan this, it just happened that way.

Over the twelve months I have been lead by my guides through a series of steps, from fluoride, DMT, pinecones, pineal gland and many other things which I feel unnecessary to mention at this point in time. Slowly I have been lead through the stages and throughout the journey I have wondered what does it mean to have your eyes opened, opened to what, that we are not alone, that we are letting the wool be pulled over our eyes, that we are giving up our divine inheritance, our true connection to ourselves. I have allowed my guide to enlighten me and thus freeing me, as he mentioned years ago. As I write the words I feel myself drifting outside my body, the air around me thickens and time seems to slow down, I am within the glimpse, that place where the world around you scurries by, and you drift with ease through life receiving everything that you need and being truly connected. I hope that the feelings I feel are somehow transmitted to you as you read the words so that you can experience the true connection for yourself. Start by making an effort to clean up your life, respect your body, respect your soul, trust that you do have guidance and they will guide you through, ask them to help you, take back your divine powers, your birthright and divine inheritance. The examples given in the abundance chapter are not just a way of manifesting money, the underlying reason that the chapter remains is to show you to not have fear, trust and love and know that you will be provided for, but you must have the connection and you must believe. As the saying goes "in the land of the blind, the one eyed man is king", will you continue to be blind or will you be guided to the light.